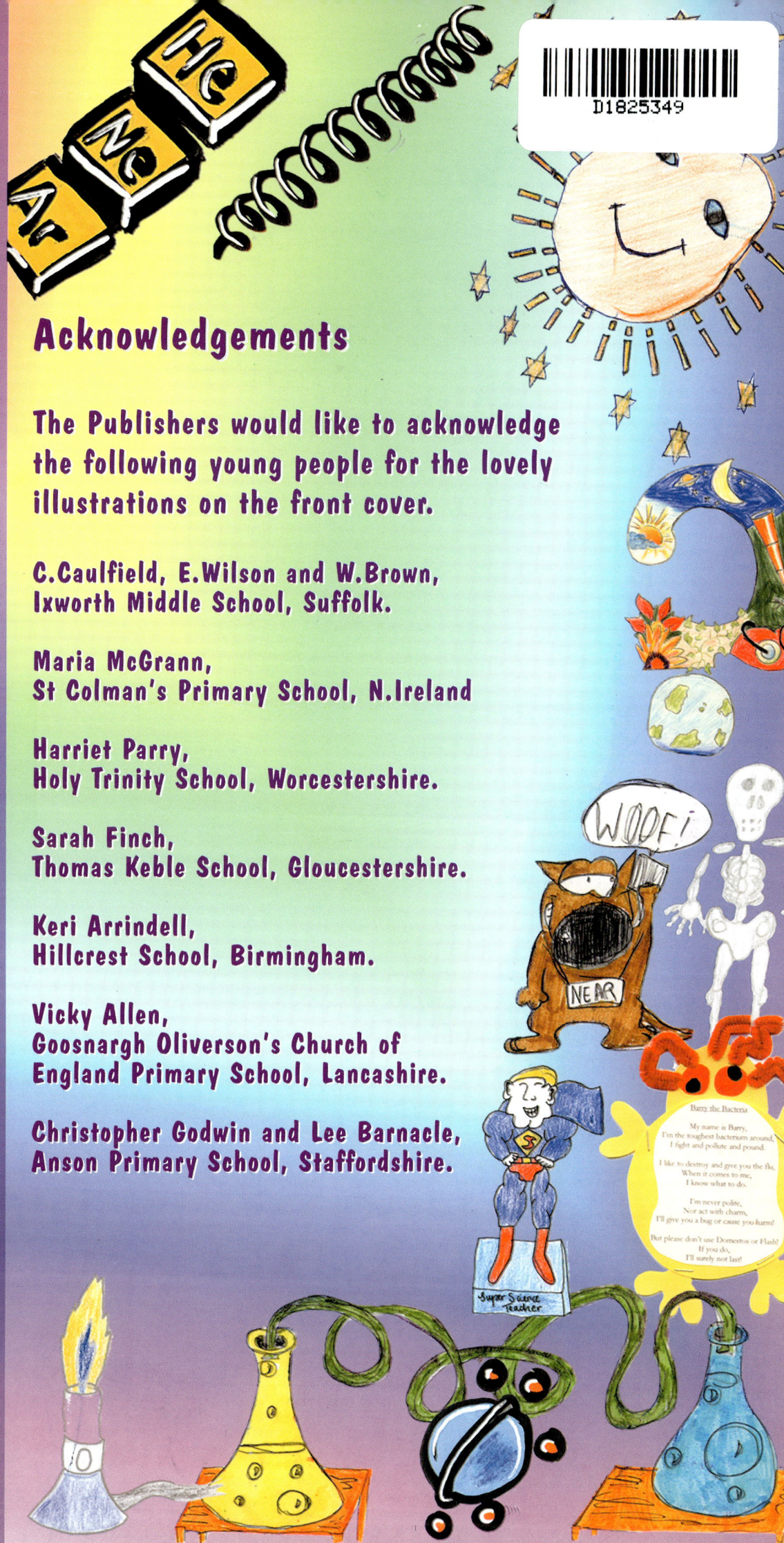

Science is Like a Tub of Ice Cream Cool and Fun!

Acknowledgements

The Publishers would like to acknowledge the following young people for the lovely illustrations on the front cover.

C.Caulfield, E.Wilson and W.Brown,
Ixworth Middle School, Suffolk.

Maria McGrann,
St Colman's Primary School, N.Ireland

Harriet Parry,
Holy Trinity School, Worcestershire.

Sarah Finch,
Thomas Keble School, Gloucestershire.

Keri Arrindell,
Hillcrest School, Birmingham.

Vicky Allen,
Goosnargh Oliverson's Church of England Primary School, Lancashire.

Christopher Godwin and Lee Barnacle,
Anson Primary School, Staffordshire.

D1825349

WOOF!

NEAR

Super Science Teacher

Barry the Bacteria

My name is Barry,
I'm the toughest bacterium around.
I fight and pollute and pound.

I like to destroy and give you the flu,
When it comes to me,
I know what to do.

I'm never polite,
Nor act with charm,
I'll give you a bug or cause you harm!

But please don't use Domestos or Flash!
If you do,
I'll surely not last!

Pfizer

100 yrs

Published by the Association for Science Education,
College Lane, Hatfield, Herts AL10 9AA

Website: http://www.ase.org.co.uk

Tel: 01707 283000
Fax: 01707 266532

Layout by Commercial Campaigns Pageplan

Printed by Streets Printers, Royston Road, Baldock, SG7 6NW

ISBN: 0 86357 322 3

Science is Like a Tub of Ice Cream – Cool and Fun

A collection of

100

Science Poems by
Primary and Secondary
School Children

Edited By Rosemary Feasey

Foreword

It gives me great pleasure to introduce this book of poetry compiled by the Association for Science Education (ASE) as part of the celebrations for its centenary in 2001. This is very appropriate in the Year of Science and an imaginative way of linking creativity with scientific exploration - the renaissance in the new century!

I was tempted to write the foreword in verse but when I read the quality of poems provided by the children I quickly abandoned the idea. The standard of the poems is superb and helps to illustrate not only children's enjoyment of science, but also the very high quality of poetry skills in the classroom. Certainly they show the clear links in terms of creativity between the sciences and the arts. The poems are a wonderful opportunity to celebrate science, language and the creative ability of young people.

As we develop a more flexible National Curriculum, we want to place the importance of a creative and cultural education at its centre. It is wonderful how children have used their imagination and creativity to express their love of science. This is just a small selection of over 13,000 poems entered and I hope that you will enjoy reading them as I have.

Finally, I would like to congratulate the ASE on their centenary and thank them for the contribution they have made to science education over the years.

Rt Hon David Blunkett MP
Secretary of State for Education and Employment

I am very pleased to be able to offer my contribution, albeit in prose, to this book of poems. Pfizer recognises the importance of fostering an interest in science in our young people and this book represents an excellent opportunity for children to express their interest in science in a very creative way.

The request for a "poem about science" has resulted in very diverse subjects being tackled in both humorous and serious ways. There are poems ranging from inventors to molecular structures to puberty; all are quite exceptional and highly imaginative.

The furtherance of science education has long been one of Pfizer's goals, so we are delighted that the Government has decreed that the academic year beginning September 2001 is to be the Year of Science. Our company continually encourages the teaching of science in schools and we contribute widely through funding and other means to show science as an interesting, lively and fun subject and we welcome the Government's initiative next year.

When we first discussed supporting the project in November 1999, no-one could have imagined that it would result in nearly 13,000 entries from children of all ages from all over the country. I congratulate all those who worked on the project and saw it through to the publication of 'Science is Like a Tub of Ice Cream, Cool and Fun'.

David McGibney
Senior Vice-President, Pfizer Global Research and Development
and Director, Sandwich Laboratories

A special thanks to Marion Frame and her pupils at St Thomas More RC Primary School, Durham. Their poems were used to inspire other children to enter the competition.

The Mysterious World of Science

The world is such a mysterious place,
From deepest ocean to outer space.
From skeletons, muscles and circulation
To melting, freezing and evaporation.
How does the earth spin
round and round?
Which is faster Light or sound
Warming up and cooling down,
Adapting to the world around.
Science is a wonderful topic,
Helping to understand the LARGE
and the microscopic.

By Francesca Turner

Science at School

Science is fun,
science is cool
I like science
at my school.
We measure the weight,
and the forces too,
So I like science at my school.

Science is fun, science is cool.
I like science at my school.
We write up experiments,
And record our results,
So I like science at my school.

By Richard Beaumont

I know sometimes
I act like a fool,
But I like science
at my school.
Although I'm not
always the best,
To make new discovery
is my quest.
So I hope
this poem pleases,
When I discover
a cure for all diseases.

By Jack Masters

When we do science
we discover,
About nature
and each other.
Some experiments are
done in the classroom,
But not yet a one
that goes boom!
Remember be cool,
don't act the fool.
When doing science at
St Thomas More School

By Martin Crouch

Happy Anniversary Science

'Good morning dear,I just got the post,
there was an invite from Science.'
'Really?What is it celebrating,dear?'
'Its celebrating a hundred years of teaching in schools.'

'What's it doing for its anniversary,dear?'
'It's holding a big bash with a G.M. cake,
and fun party games like 'pass the particle'.
Its inviting old friends:Thomas Edison, Albert
Einstein,Louie Pasteur.'

' What should we get him ,chemistery set?'
'Isn't that a bit predictable,dear?'
'I hear black holes are quite fun.'
'Too expensive,dear and if they suck in matter how
are we supposed to wrap it?'

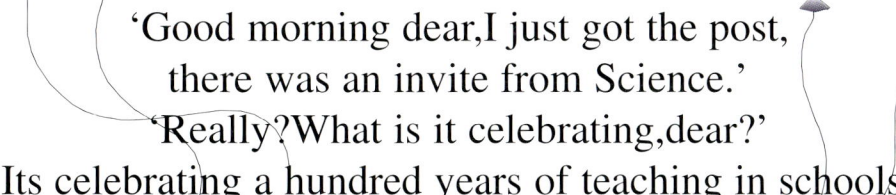

Jules Williams, age 14, Reigate Grammar School, Surrey

We like experiments

They are fun.

Testing, guessing what's going on.

Will it melt?

Will it grow?

Will it explode?

We hope so!

We like Science

It is great.

Let's sing and dance and celebrate.

Class One, ages 5 and 6, Monkton Primary School, Kent

A Light bulb

Domesticated
version of a lightning bug,
Without its wings on

Alden Davis, age 12, Southbank International School, London

An alien sends home a Letter

Dear Planet Mars,
I have arrived secure on Planet Earth,
Where Human beings are very peculiar,
I went to investigate this place called school,
Upon me came a 'lesson' named Science!

Diminutive humans set conflagration to liquids and solids,
They exercise their minds with words and pictures,
The leader gives out commands,
Others observe and obey him or her!

Now assembled is an experiment,
Where specific protection is worn,
Hazardous liquids and substances are given out,
Along with plants and granites!

I can see minor explosions,
Dotted around the room,
After the information wrote down,
Things are packed up and disentangled!

Familiar humans leaving,
Unfamiliar humans arriving,
Leader still at the front,
I abandon this mirthful environment!

Humans are very bizarre and do extraordinary things,
I must confess that I take pleasure from that 'lesson' named Science!

Your Peace
Captain Martian

Catherine Stewart, age 13, Thomas Telford School, Shropshire

THE RAT

Once when someone let out the rat

our science teacher screamed like a cat

it ran right up the teacher's leg

she jumped about and then grabbed a peg

she hit it quick

then with one sharp prick

the rat lay flat

on a heatproof mat

and it's been there ever since

aah! That's how the dinner ladies make the mince

Laura Mulvee, age 11, Loreto Grammar School, Altringham

Science

Science, Science it's so great
That's why I never turn up late
It really brightens up my week
Yes, Science really is my peak

Biology, Physics Chemistry too
Grass is green and cows go moo
Sex education is such fun
Found out that I came from my mum

Science really is the best
It's so much better than all the rest
If there was only one subject I could do
It would be Science I assure you

Jonathan McCarthy, age 14, Trinity Catholic High School, Woodford, Essex

SCIENTISTS

Newton discovered gravity
While sitting under an apple tree.
Archimedes had a good laugh
Whilst water poured over the edge of his bath.

Jenner a vaccine he wanted to find
To leave the smallpox forever behind.
Fleming thought he was extremely bold
Leaving his bacteria to turn into mould.

All of these scientists have helped me and you
Because of the things they managed to do.
And many others there will surely be
Perhaps the next will be you or me!

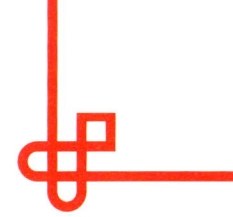

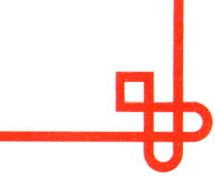

Nadia Williamson, age 9, Ursuline Convent Preparatory School, Wimbledon, London

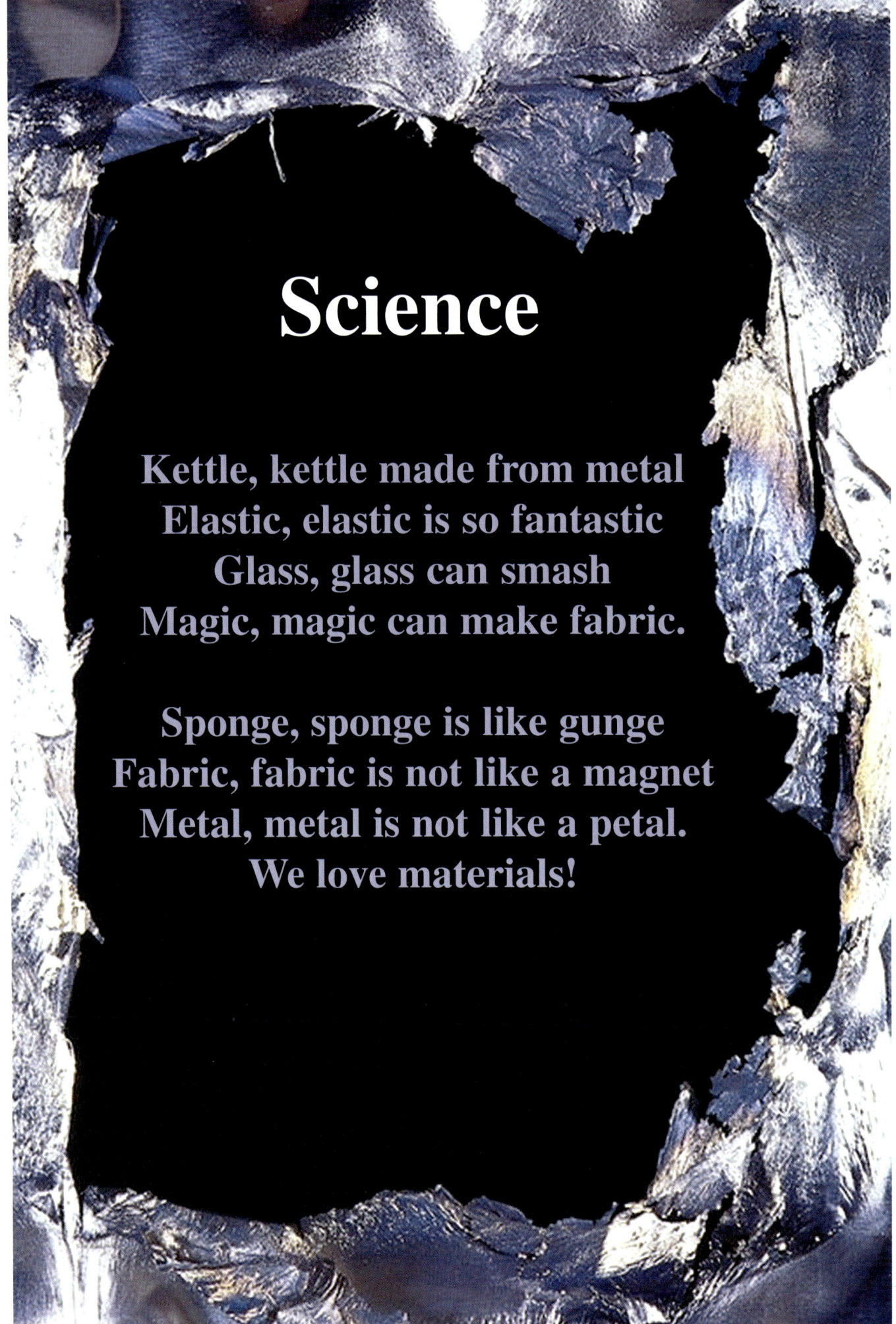

Science

Kettle, kettle made from metal
Elastic, elastic is so fantastic
Glass, glass can smash
Magic, magic can make fabric.

Sponge, sponge is like gunge
Fabric, fabric is not like a magnet
Metal, metal is not like a petal.
We love materials!

Stephanie Robe and Philippa Ogden, age 5, Ashley Primary School, South Shields, Tyne & Wear

And She Would Remember......

Later she would recall
Her mother's gentle humming,
The heat of the sun on her shoulders
The sound of bluetits chirping among the branches/
How heavy the air, as if filled with invisible weights
How when she opened her eyes she saw the firey glow over the roof

The way the inner shell holds two electrons
Expanding, increasing outwards,
Unleashing the energy it holds,
And across the firey background
A phoenix seemed to shoot across
Exploding into giant white stars,
That is the battle for oxygen,
Iron against all powerful aluminium
Sodium snatching away at feeble zinc

And she would remember
Once leafy green trees,
Reduced to ashes and charcoal,
The carbon remains floating
Upwards on the heavy air
And the clouds of black smoke
Rising and billowing,
Blocking out the delicate wisps of white cloud,
Pushing the residue ever upwards
To be snatched at by the will o' the wisp wind,

And how the childs features distorted
Into a picture of terror,
His feet rooted to the ground
His brain unable to send the necessary signals through his cells

And she would remember
How he turned and ran
Stumbling on his short legs
Screaming from the bottom of his lungs,
The vacuum that is there
Emptying his aveoli of all air

And this her brother's teddy
Rid of it's filling,
Empty.....

Rose Ganly, age 14, Heanor Gate School, Derbyshire

Experiment

At school we're doing growing things
with cress,
sprinkly seeds in plastic pots
of cotton wool.

Jenny's cress sits up on the sill
she gives it water.
Mine is shut inside the cupboard
dark and dry.

Now her pot has great big clumps
of green.
Mine hasn't
Mrs Burbridge calls it science
I call it mean.

Amy Jackson, age 12, Glebelands School, Cranleigh, Surrey

It's Amazing

It's amazing how science surrounds us ,

The beauty of the animal kingdom ,

The vastness of space ,

The endless discoveries and inventions ,

It' s amazing how much we have found out about the world around us , yet we will

never stop finding out more .

It' s amazing how just one person can find out something new , and add another

chapter to a science textbook .

It's amazing how much we have evolved ,

From simple one-celled animals ,

To beings with thoughts , feelings and emotions .

It's amazing how a person from this planet ,

Can travel at incredible speed through space ,

And walk on the moon ,

Leaving footprints that will last

It's amazing how some materials can change from liquids into solids,

And back again ,

In the blink of an eye (well , almost) .

It's amazing how a force pushes us to the ground every day ,

Something we can't see makes things fall .

It's amazing .

Just amazing .

Claudia Saviotti, age 12, Lady Margaret School, Parson's Green, London

Science

The Science we do at school is Fantastic

We learn so much our brains stretch like elastic

We learnt about ears,

and all about eyes,

We've learnt about age ,

We've learnt about size,

We've measured our pulse rate and written it down,

Drew a graph and now we have found,

That running around,

Makes you heart go quicker,

And sitting down slows the old "ticker".

Static electricity makes your hair stand one end,

I rubbed the balloon over my head and then on my friend,

I watched her hair,

As it rose in the air,

And everyone else turned round to stare,

Electricity makes light bulbs blow,

Don't you know?

Well I do now,

And so do you!

Rebecca Hughes, age 10, Thames Ditton Junior School, Surrey

Recipe for a scientist

1.   Start with one normal human being.

2.   Marinade in madness for 1 hour.

3.   Stir in a strange voice.

4.   Mix hair until it stands up on end.

5.   Simmer gently in some knowledge and leave to cool.

To serve:
Place in a science lab, spoon on a lab coat and garnish with some safety goggles.

Louise Fowkes, age 13, Saint John the Baptist School, Woking, Surrey

'I WONDER WHY'

I wonder why the kettle sings,

I wonder what makes the telephone ring,

I wonder what makes plants and trees grow,

I wonder what makes ice and snow,

I wonder why flames are orange and blue,

1 wonder who invented glue,

I wonder why some things burn,

All these things I would like to learn.

Olivia Tuck, age 7, Seer Green Combined School, Beaconsfield, Buckinghamshire

Science

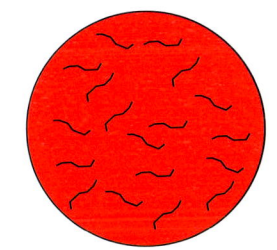

The planets all orbit the Sun,
Swirling and sparkling one by one,
Skies filled with enchanted stars,
Twisting and taunting 'round Saturn and Mars.

Down below on the damp, soft soil,
Plants and bees slave and toil,
Scattering pollen and clustering petals,
    Flaunting their leaves, seedlings and sepals.

    Messages to and from the brain,
    Shoot round the body again and again,
    Labouring muscles stretch and groan,
    Skin and flesh surrounds crumbling bone.

Frequencies waver, ripple and rise,
    Light reflects and shoots into our eyes,
        Sound waves hum with pitch and vibration,
            Our eyes seek to find, with keen exploration.

        Science is everywhere, in space and on Earth,
        Bodies strain for all they are worth.
        Scientist explore microscopic places,
        Skins and cells and people's faces.

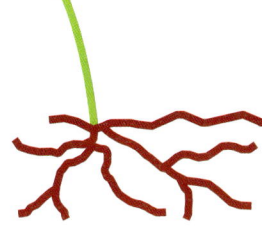

Charlotte Green, age 11, Thames Ditton Junior School, Surrey

Science is fun

Lightning flashes
Then comes the sound
It,s thunder
I,ll be bound
Light is faster
Than the sound

Jake Phillip, age 7, Epsom County Primary School, Surrey

The History of Science

1. **Archimedes** was ambitious;
His ambitions gave Science birth:
'Give me a lever long enough
And I will move the Earth.'

2. The Sun rises in the morning,
It goes to bed at night,
But **Copernicus** said that was wrong,
And Copernicus was right.

3. Kepler visited astronomers,
He went on many trips,
But it still took him years to realise
A planet's orbit is an ellipse.

4. The Church didn't like what **Galileo** said
Their threats chilled him to the bone,
So that he denied what his telescope saw,
Though he said 'they move' in an undertone.

5. **Newton** watched an apple fall'
And Newton really cared,
That gravity attracts
But inverse to distance squared.

6. **Darwin** voyaged on *The Beagle*,
He came back feeling limp:
He had found his great great grandfather
Was descended from a chimp.

7. **Bell** was a great inventor
But it only made him ill:
He made the first telephone call,
And received the first telephone bill.

8. **Einstein** looked at his page of notes,
He wondered, scratched his head and stared:
If his working out was right,
It showed e = mc squared.

9. **Heisenberg** was uncertain,
Scientists would lose face:
Since when they measured quanta
They had to choose between speed or place.

10. **Crick and Watson** worked as a pair,
They worked out what to say:
They drew a double helix
And called it DNA.

Hannah Brown, age 12, Christ's Hospital School, Horsham, Sussex

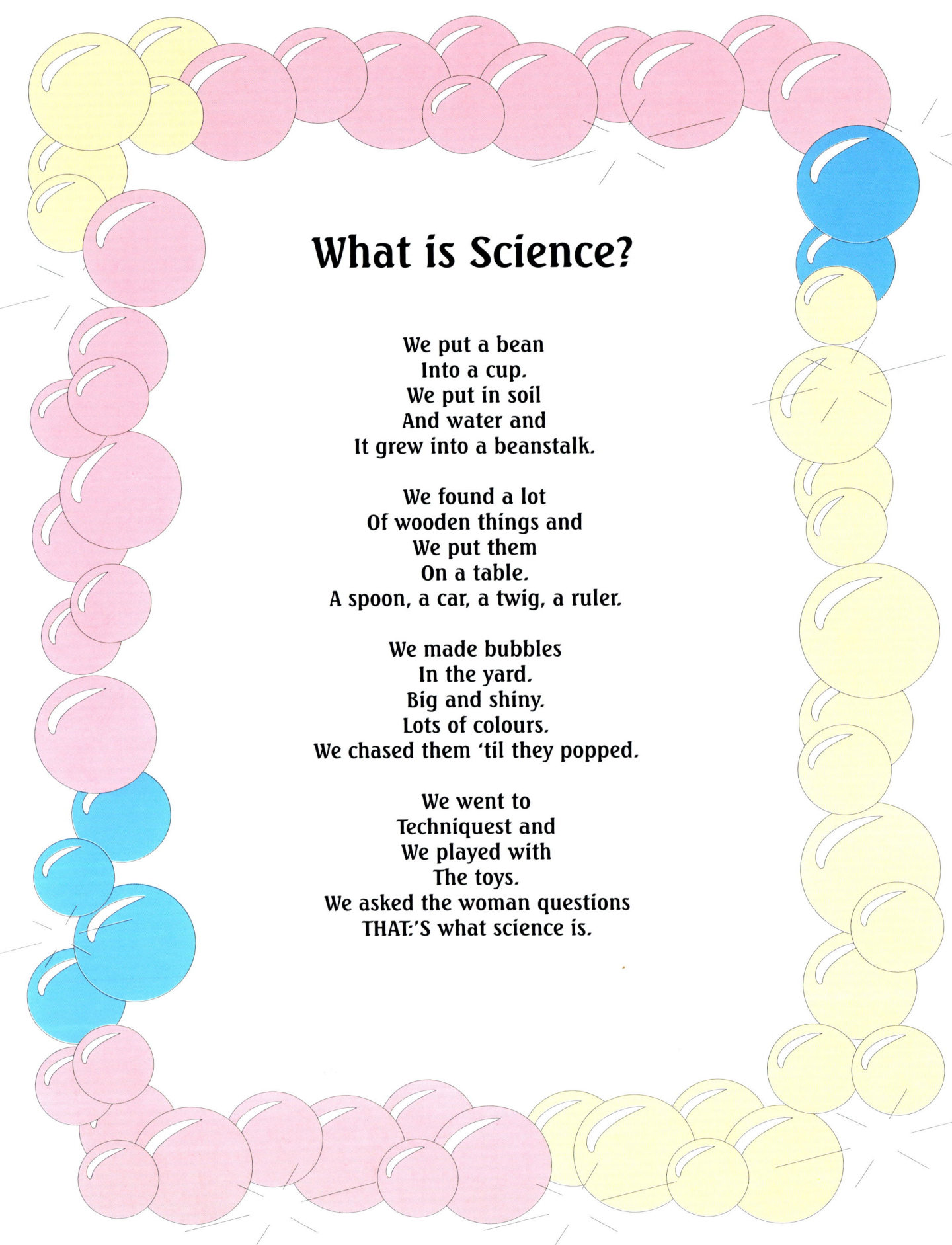

What is Science?

We put a bean
Into a cup.
We put in soil
And water and
It grew into a beanstalk.

We found a lot
Of wooden things and
We put them
On a table.
A spoon, a car, a twig, a ruler.

We made bubbles
In the yard.
Big and shiny.
Lots of colours.
We chased them 'til they popped.

We went to
Techniquest and
We played with
The toys.
We asked the woman questions
THAT:'S what science is.

Miss Carey's Special Needs Class, age 5 and 6, Graig Y Wion Primary School, Mid Glamorgan

Science is so much fun

It's like eating a currant bun!

Science is really great

You learn a lot about weight.

There's lots to do and lots to see

You can even examine a pea.

We have learnt about dark and light

It has made us very bright.

Science is really good

It is better than sawing wood.

So learn about science today

and make your teacher's day!

Thomas Fariman, age 4, Our Lady Immaculate School, Tolworth, Surrey

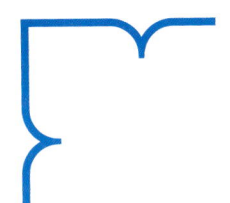

Boat Rap

In our Science Lesson we had a boat,
Hoping on the guttering it will float,
We timed it on the stopwatch when we tested it out,
And the long thin boat swam like a trout.

We turned the fan on medium power,
Looking at if all the boats would stay straight like a flower
My boat's mast wasn't tall,
and I thought it was going to fall.

The best boat was Charlotte's boat,
and it swam like water going down your throat.

Our results showed that a tall mast,
would never last,
and a big sail, would defiantly fail,
but a short mast, would defiantly last,
and a small sail, would never fail!!

Mahima Charan, age 9, Chalkwell Hall Junior School, Leigh-on-Sea, Essex

THE SCIENCE AUCTION

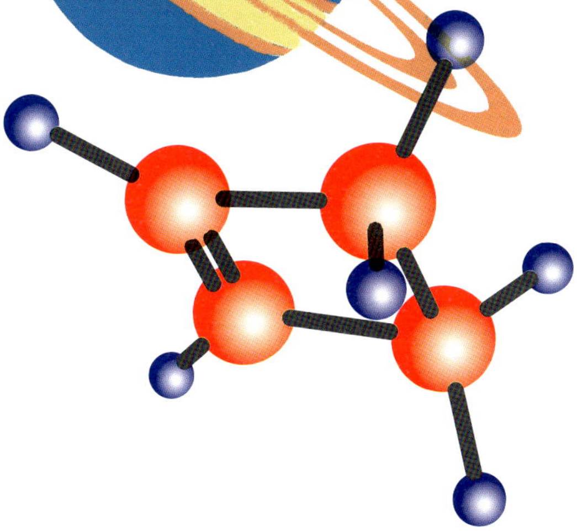

First of all in lot No.1,
A model of Saturn which revolves round the sun.
Lot No.2, the next in line,
An exciting substance of alkaline.
Moving on to lot No.3,
An interesting read on biology.
And lot No.4 is sure to excite,
An invention on Edison to give us light.
In lot No.5, an intriguing addition,
A strange world without gravity or friction.
Lot No.6 deserves a mention,
Marconi's radio, a worthy invention.
Lot No.7 is defiantly worth it,
A well put together parallel circuit.
Lot No.8 is a body that grows,
A heart, a mouth and five pairs of toes.
Plants are growing in lot No.9,
They need water and lots of sunshine.
Lot No.10, a CD ROM,

GOING. GOING. GOING. GONE!

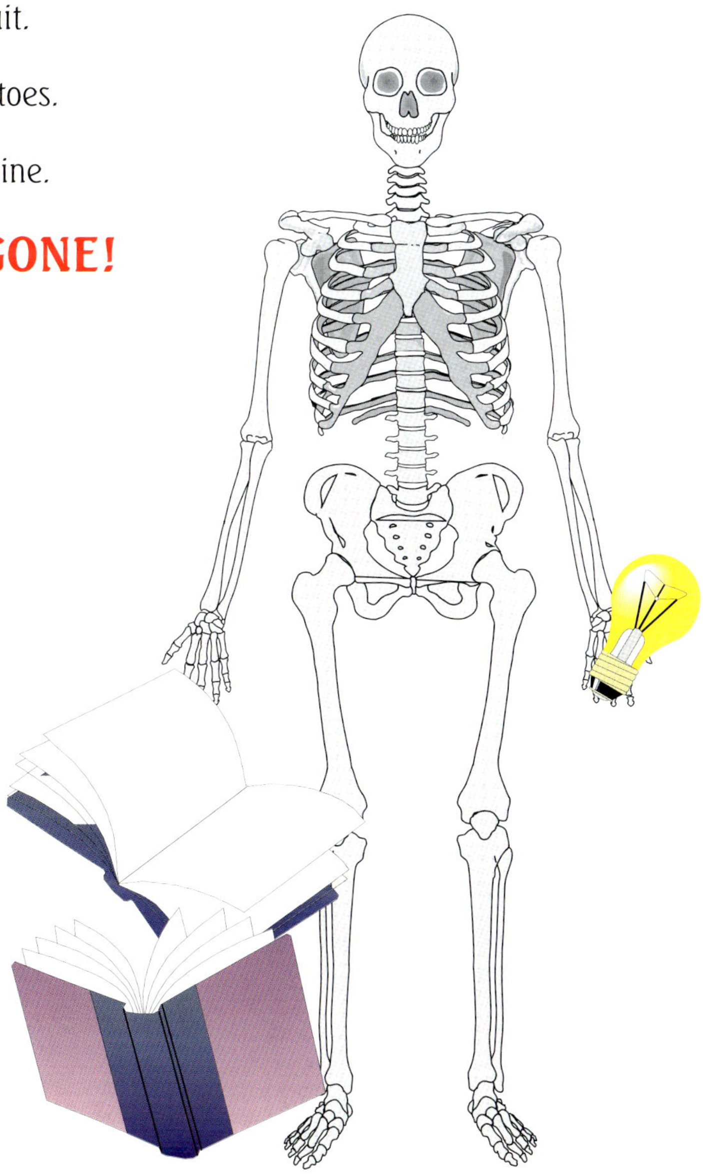

Charlotte Lindsay and Alison Johnson, age 13, Uplands Community College, East Sussex

Science

I played with magnets

At school.

I don't like science.

Dana Porter, age 5, St Mary's Catholic Primary School, Cannock, Staffordshire

Waterloo

Some people spend a penny
Some people need a tiddle,
Girls are very neat, sitting on the seat
And boys just make a puddle.

It's sometimes called a "John"
That's American to you.
We have "Loo" and "Lav",
Now you've met your Waterloo!

Some loos have a handle
A button or a chain,
We will sit for hours in constipated pain.

Toilet tissue now is pretty, soft and fun,
But in the olden days, you got newsprint on your bum!

Please don't think I'm rude, or mad as a hatter
But when you use the loo,
Give thanks to Thomas Crapper!

Sarah Peart, age 10, Ixworth Middle School, Suffolk

A JOURNEY THROUGH SCIENCE!

From gravity, a muscular arm pulling objects
to the core of the earth,
To up thrust, the complete opposite,
From the tip of your hair,
To the skin on the soles of your feet,
Within lie a variety of organs, muscles,
arteries, and many other phenomenal things,
Your heart at a beat increasing and decreasing,
Your bone structure to keep you up and going,
Nails and hair a collection of dead cells,
Six superb senses to guide you round the world.

From the dull rattle of a dead bulb,
To the bright spark of an overpowered light,
From a lost and lonely wire,
To a whole circuit full of gadgetry,
Within an electrical current races through the wires,
Yet with the touch of a button all could be led to a cease,
From a series circuit, Christmas tree lights,
To a parallel circuit, the system of wiring in a house.

From oxygen, what a human needs to live and
what a plant uses in photosynthesis,
To carbon dioxide, what a plant takes in and
what we give out as a waste product,
From evaporation,
To condensation,
From melting in intense heat,
To freezing, the reverse as it is.

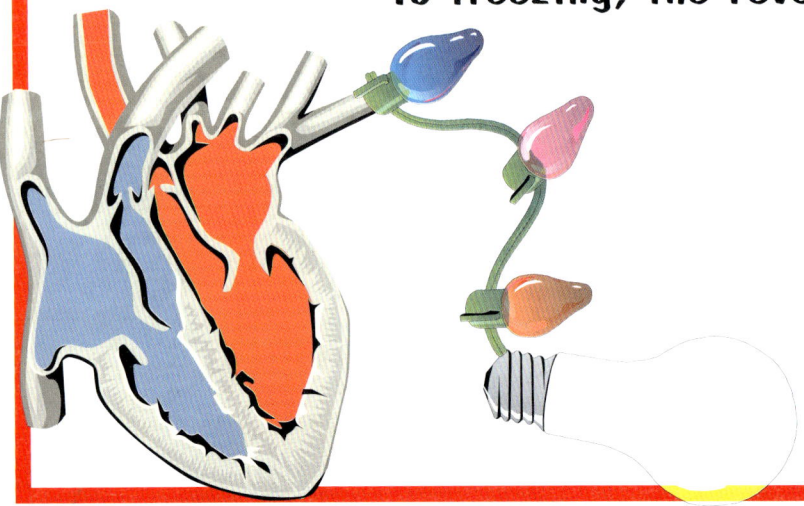

Tanya Patrick, age 10, Marshfield Primary School, Cardiff

Water Balloon

Water balloon,
Full of liquid
Heavy but bouncy,
Rolling over and over,
Strong and bendy and
stretchy,
Squeeze it,
Bounce it,
Running away.
Pin it,
Water squirting like a
fountain,
Pop and it was gone.

Reception Group, age 5, Queensway Catholic Primary School, Torquay, Devon

sunny days

golden

rays

flaming

flower

rustling leaves

pushing up

straight stem

little shoot

stripy seed

A sunflower starts here

Hannah Eshelby and friends, age 6 and 7, Stancliffe Hall School, Darley Dale, Derbyshire

"All I Want Is A Cold Fizzy Drink "

The geek strolled up to the counter after a hard days swatting,
The cheery woman popped up her head,
"How can I help you ?"
"Please could I purchase some chilled pressurised carbonic acid."
"Eh, I didn't quite catch that."
"Please could I purchase some chilled pressurised carbonic acid."
"What! ?"
"Please .... could .... I .... purchase .... some .... chilled .... pressurised
.... carbonic .... acid."
"I only speak English !"
"Well all I want is a cold fizzy drink."
"Thank you. Should have said that in the first place. Well that will be a
large heptagonal silver coin, a smaller heptagonal silver coin and a very
small circular coin."
"Pardon!"
"75p please! And I shall put these silver coins into my very advanced,
digital, electronic, monitory system."
"Eh!"
"You're not the only one good at science you know."

Rachel Locke, age 11, Coed-Y-Lan Primary School, Pontypridd

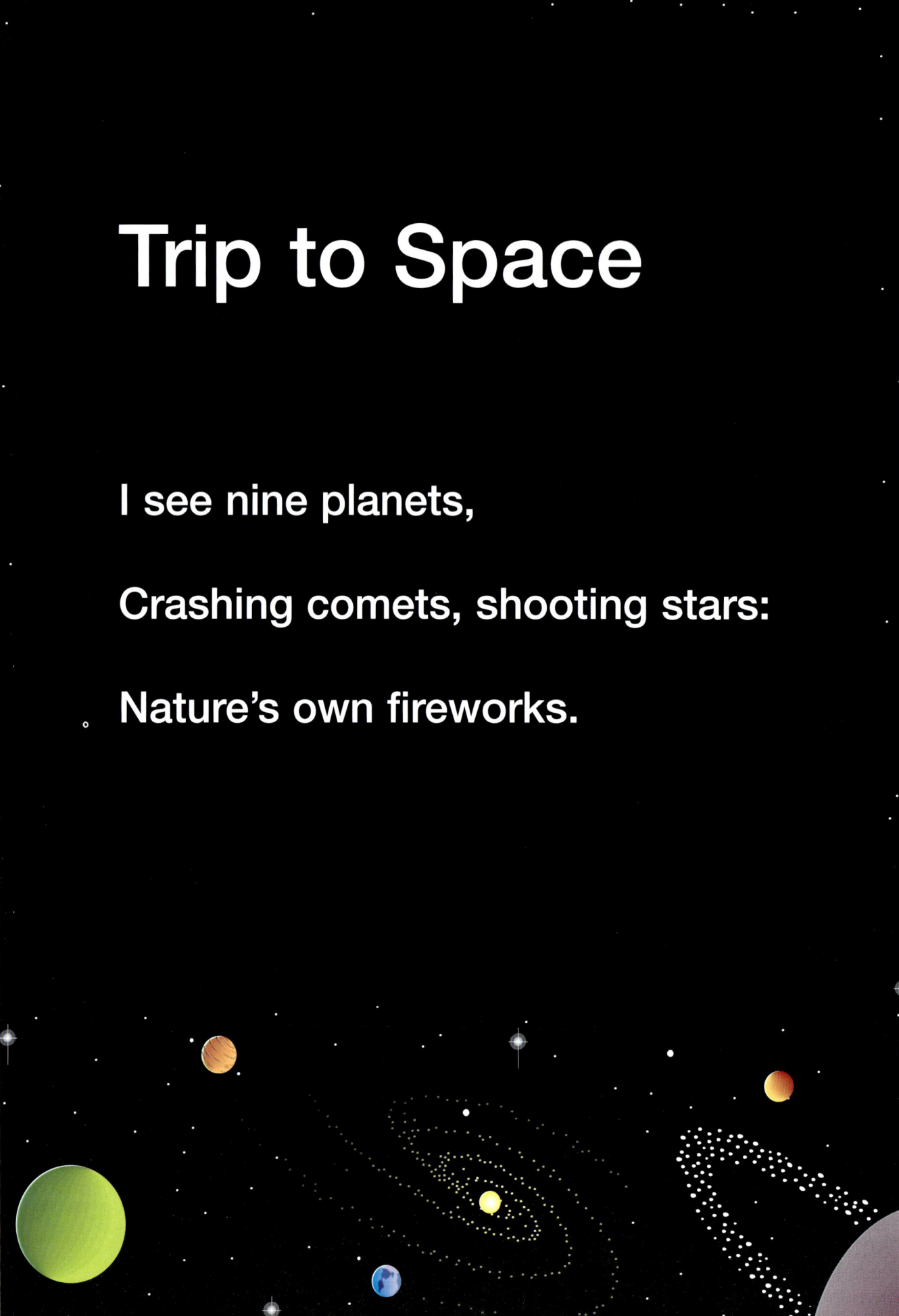

Trip to Space

I see nine planets,

Crashing comets, shooting stars:

Nature's own fireworks.

Tamsin Edwards and Dominique Forrest, age 9, Polam Hall Junior School, Darlington, Co. Durham

What do Scientists do Dad?

What do Scientists do Dad?
I don't know – they don't explain.
It's finding ways of stopping pain,
And sorting out Acid Rain.

What do Scientists do Dad?
I don t know – it's all solutions
Things like answers to pollution
And solving the puzzle of evolution.

What do Scientists do Dad?
Is it all new ways of phoning?
Or more about animal cloning –
perhaps stopping global warming.

What do Scientists do Dad?
I don't know – don't they save trees?
Final cures for all disease,
And remove poisons from the seas.

What do Scientists do Dad?
It's about the future of the human race,
Exploring possibilities of life in space
and finding new types of GM maize.

Wow! I want to be a Scientist when I grow up!!!

Louisa Cantwell, age 7, Cokethorpe School, Witney, Oxfordshire

Not all Chemists Wear White Coats

It's Tuesday afternoon, just before two,
We're making our way up to F22.
Practicals come but just once a week,
Let's hope this time my burette doesn't leak!

With Bunsen burners lit we're raring to go
And already I've spilt acid - Oh no!
A big brown stain is starting to appear,
I wanted my lab coat white all year.

Dr. Gwyther's coming I must try my best,
Since I did really badly in yesterday's test.
I pretend she's not there and try to stay calm,
But indicator leaks all over my arm!
Combined with the acid my lab coat's a mess,
But I keep working hard just trying to impress.

Just ten minutes left and things have gone well,
I might even finish before the bell.
I'm glad my results did not depend
On the state of my lab coat at the end.
It's brown in places and orange too,
As well as green, purple, yellow and blue

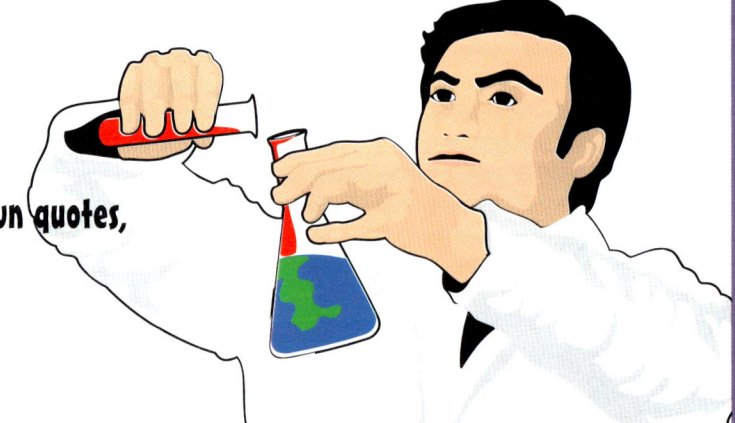

Well I've certainly proved the well known quotes,
That not all chemists wear white coats!

J. Bowen, A. Nicolls, H. Maslin, E. Bradley, age 16 and 17, Colchester County High School, Essex

WHAT I LIKE ABOUT SCIENCE....

Look round the Science Room, what do I see ?
Conduction, refraction, reflection, convection,
But what do they mean to me ?

Looking at galaxy, gravity, energy,
Uncover worlds that are new to me.
Oxygen, hydrogen, what do they mean ?
And photosynthesis, what can that be ?
Science can help me to solve the puzzle,
Science can help me to turn the key.

Telescopes, microscopes, scientific words,
Trees, leaves and nature, strange names of birds.
Do cogs and levers have anything the same ?
Vitamins and minerals each have a name.
Moisture and pressure are different things.
Crystals which start up in mines and end up in rings.
Science is great, Science is fun,
Science is brilliant for <u>everyone!</u>

Discover why water gushes through drains,
Discover why blood runs through my veins
Voltmeter, friction, new things to learn about.
Ideas for experiments swim through our brains.
Some people ask me why I like Science,
In Science no lesson is ever the same.

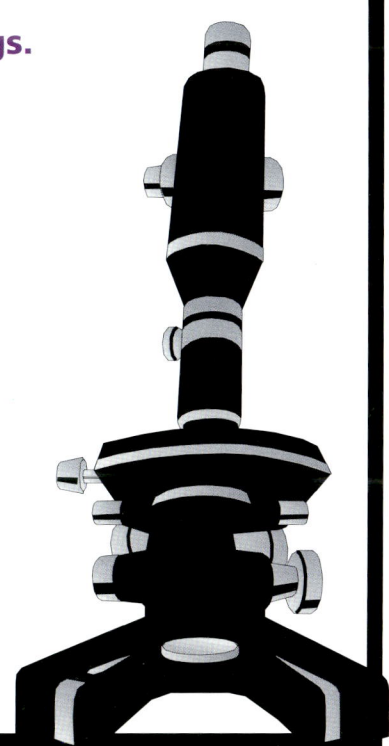

Olivia Robey, age 8, The Cavendish School, Camden, London

Science

Push pull
Turn around,
Forces can make things
Touch the ground.

Forces are strong
Forces are light
The wind blows
Even at night

Science!

Science is all about learning
Of things like forces and evaporation.
We are planting seeds at the moment
And we've learned about condensation.

Does sound travel faster than air,
Or do plants need water to grow.
Which kind of flowers are poisonous,
And do they germinate high or low.

I know the three states of matter,
Which are solid, liquid and gas.
The temperature outside could be hot or cold
And the quantity of an object is the mass.

We've been taught the order of the planets.
The moon the sun and the stars.
We have also learnt about technology,
And that there didn' t use to be cars!

Electricity is a clever thing.
We use it for almost everything.
Gravity is the force that pulls us down.
How did I know that ... from Mrs Brown!

Emily Henning, age 10, Burgess Hill School, West Sussex

Electrical Loop

I start in POSITIVE
Through to Negative
I have great trouble
Compacting myself into the connecting Wire.

O, No, I'm entering the bulb
The filament its to small
I'm so hot!
I'm burning up!
I'm glowing red!

Phew! I'm back in the wire
But I'm still squashed

I'm back in POSITIVE
through to negative again.
I'm SLOWING down.
They broke the circuit!
I can't move till they complete
the loop and send me flying
Round the cell, bulb and
connecting wire.

● = Me

─── = My course

Charlie Crow, age 11, Bushmead Junior School, Luton, Beds

A Conversation about Science

Science is boring,
Science makes me moan.
It's all about chemicals,
Atoms and bones.
Science teachers are crazy,
They're really quite troubling,
Gazing at chemicals
Fizzing and bubbling,
Making a fuss about
Forces and sound-
Who cares what makes you
Stay on the ground?
In my opinion,
Science is no fun.
I'd rather be painting
Than studying the sun.

Oh no! What you're saying
Is absolute nonsense!
Science is fun but
Important, for instance,
Would you be here If
The Sun didn't shine,
Or if the planets travelled
In a straight line?
What about the laws
Of evolution,
Or why there is So much
pollution?
So you see, Science is
Not to be sniffed at –
If it wasn't for Science
You'd be non-existant!

Caroline Laing, age 14, Rosebery School, Epsom, Surrey

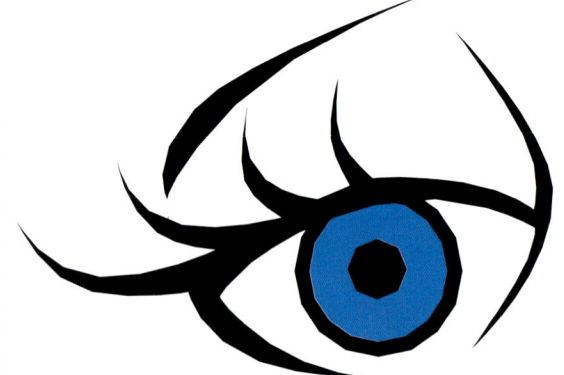 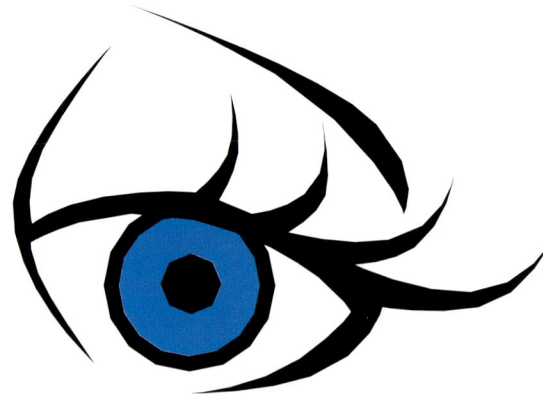

Eyes
Looking, blinking,
Gleaming, crying, smiling
shining stars

THE MYSTERIOUS WORLD OF SCIENCE

Seeds grow into flowers,
Caterpillars turn into butterflies,
Ice melts into water,
Eggs hatch into chicks,
Nuts grow into trees,
Caitlin grows up,
Everything is science!!!!!

Caitlin Boyle, age 6, St Anthonys Catholic Primary School, Dulwich, London

What if...

What if
We didn't have light
Could we live in darkness?

What if
There was no Gravity,
Could we live in space?

What if there was no oxygen,
Could we still be alive?

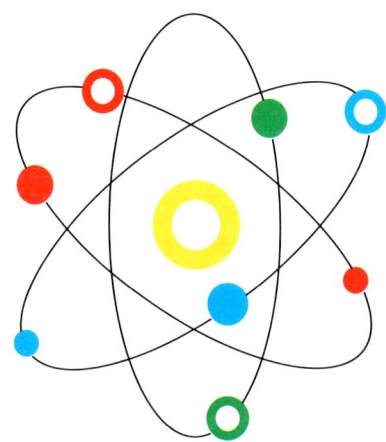

What if
A giant meteor collided into the Earth,
Could anything survive?

Ruth Weaver, age 11, St Mary's Catholic School, Penzance, Cornwall

scientists ask questions
scientists find answers

Jack Gregory and friends, age 6 and 7, Stancliffe Hall School, Darley Dale, Derbyshire

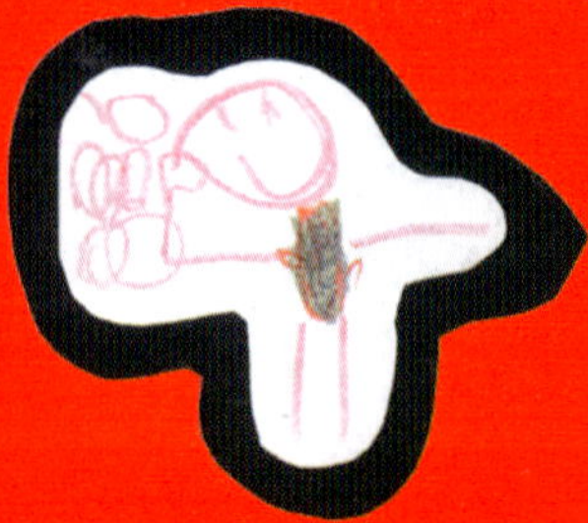

We Like Science!

We like Science!
In Science we blow bubbles, (Pretend to blow a bubb
In Science we watch bubbles. (Pretend to watch bub
Bubbles are round, (Make a circle with fingers)
Bubbles are sticky, (Rub hands together)
Bubbles float and fly, (Pretend to fly)
Bubbles POP! (Clap on 'POP')

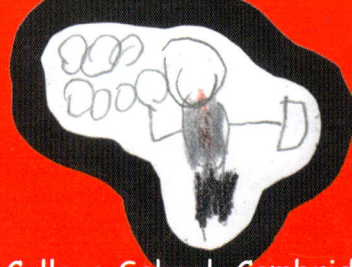

Kindergarten L, age 5, St John's College School, Cambridge

The Science Lab

Everyones scared of the Science Lab
"Its scary in there" they say
But I don't believe one word
That these little children say.

You see I've been in that Science Lab
And you'll be surprised to hear
That all screams are of delight
Where from the children who got their experiments right.

If you had been in that Science Lab
It would be clear to see.
That everything in that Science Lab
Is as easy as 1,2,3

The teacher has taught me a lot
About atoms,compounds and mixtures
About digestives, system, cells and Breathing
And light and prims
But best thing I learned is not to be scared of
THE SCIENCE LAB

Emma Taylor, age 12, Thornhill College, Derry, N. Ireland

Germs

I am a little germ
I can make you very sick
I swim around your insides
And multiply real quick

I come with different diseases
Through the wind and on your hands
And I fight with your immune system
I am no fan of man

Once I 'm in your body
You need the doctors help
He has the magic potion
That helps you flush me out

I hate all antibiotics
Penicillin is the worst
But the best way to avoid me
Is to consider your body first

Drink plenty of fresh water
Eat healthy food each day
And don't forget you need to sleep
As well as enjoying play

Sarah Gibbs, age 11, Porchester Community School, Fareham, Hampshire

Science

Biology, Chemistry and Physics alone,

Help us to learn about the body and bone,

Solids, liquids and gases,

Metals and their masses.

Learn what happens when a chemical reacts

Find out all the figures and facts.

What is inside a plant cell?

How do magnets attract and repel?

So to set up an experiment and see something fab,

You've got to be in a science lab!

Ruth Mansfield, age 14, Holy Trinity CE Senior School, Halifax, Yorkshire

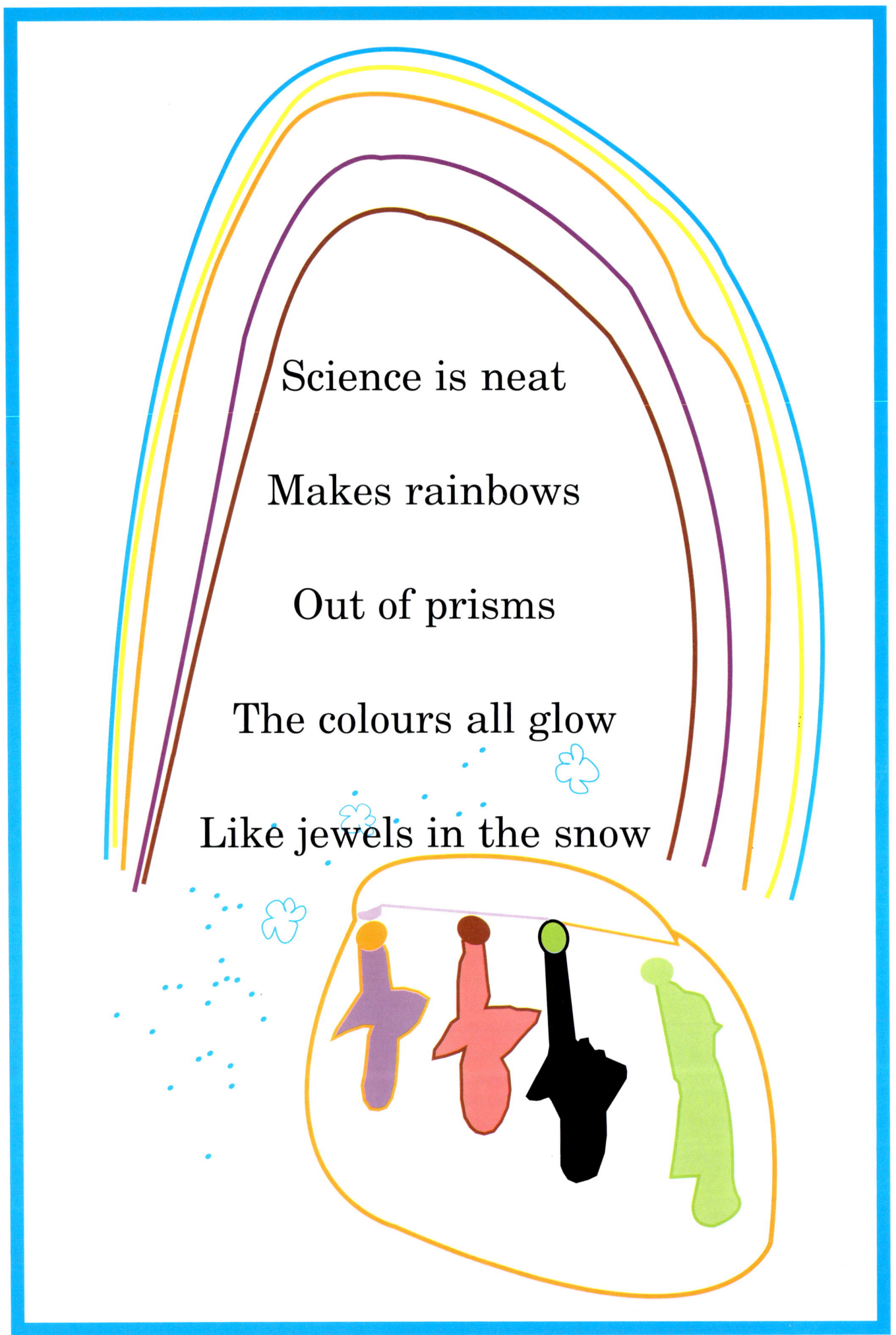

Science is neat

Makes rainbows

Out of prisms

The colours all glow

Like jewels in the snow

Katie Mundie, age 7, Cherry Trees School, Bury St Edmunds, Suffolk

What's the attraction?

Magnets are just like people,
Unlike attracts and likes repel!
Or as Mum would say,
"Opposites attract!"
And I say " That's a fact!"

For example......

My best friend and mate is Lee.I
He's really not a bit like me!

I enjoy a game of football
Lee can't bear to watch at all!

I've got the looks - _
While he's got the books!

I like the fun of adventure camp
But Lee gets excited by a stamp.

I love wrestling on T.V,
Eastenders is his cup of tea !

Different we are - like a magnet's ends,
But Lee and me - we're the best of friends!

Samantha Greaves and Kimberley Barton, age 11, The Usher Junior School, Lincoln

The Highway of life

Everyone always assumes that they have perfect control over their life,
More than once have I come across the saying "it's my life it's up to me what I do with it."
However, this I consider may not be the case,
Often have I delved in to the delicate, complex network of my brain and spent hours contemplating a thought.
The idea that before we have even developed into a diminutive embryo; barely the size of a fingernail, our life has been planned by a higher authority.
People openly except that before birth our eye colour, hair and even parts of our personality have been implanted into our genetics.
The elaborate chemical instructions of our parent's genes, carry some precise detail on how to create a human.
So how can we be so sure that planted within our bodies are not the possibilities of undiscovered networks, with the exact knowledge of the events we will encounter in our lives, whether we will marry, have children and at what age we will depart this life.
The most complicated network within us, one we experience every day.
Much like a highway, we travel the roads with a vague expectance of where it is taking us.
These roads we have no control of, there are no junctions, turn offs or hard shoulders to turn on when we desire a break from the hassles and stress.
We keep on driving that's all we can do,
Confronting the problems that appear.
You can not stop your life, even when you're unaware of it, significant, incredible things are occurring all around you.
How can we be so sure that like our eye colour, hair and personalities, our future has not also been erected before our life has even begun?

Rebecca Bamford, age 14, Heanor Gate School, Heanor, Derbyshire

A Light Experiment

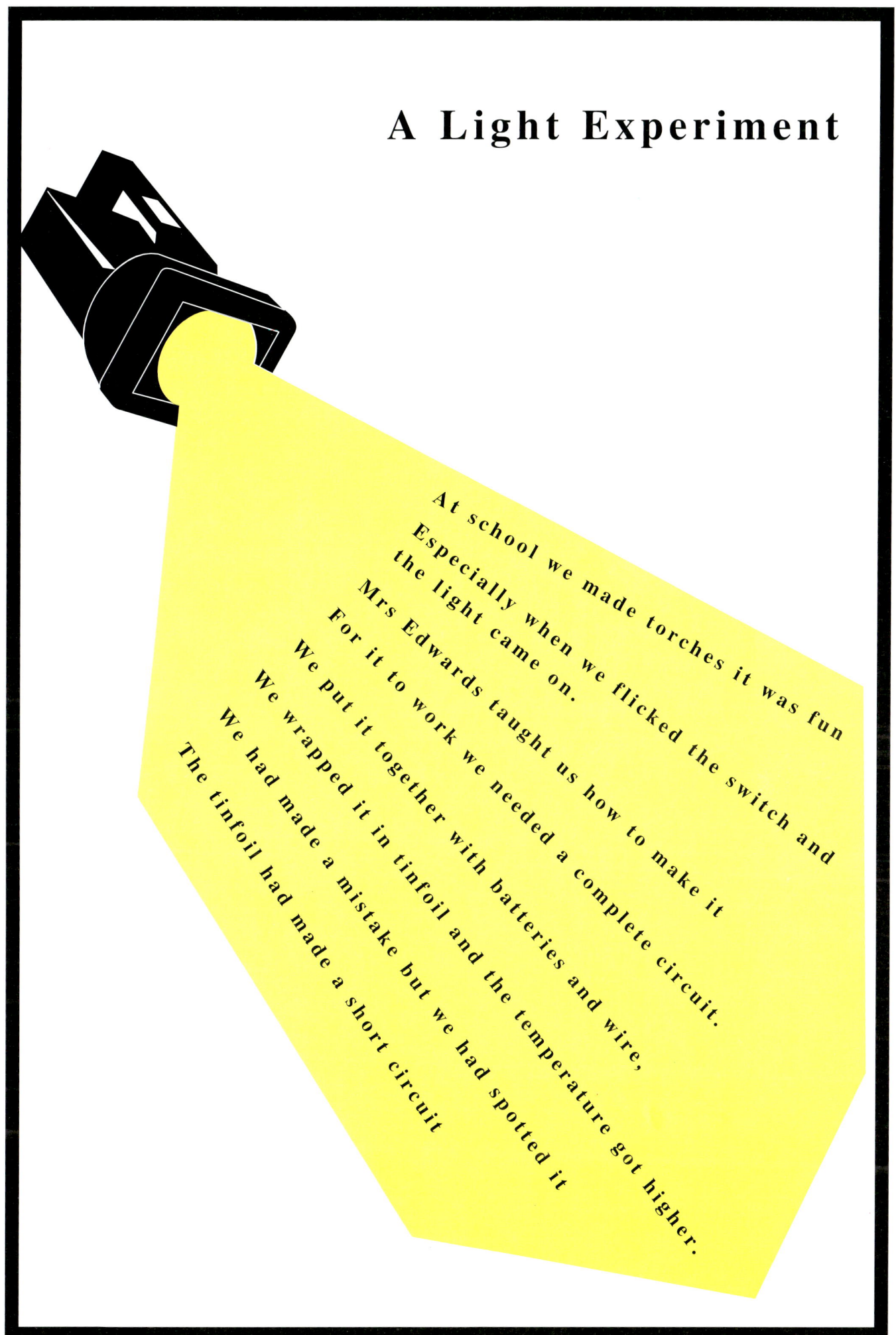

At school we made torches it was fun
Especially when we flicked the switch and
the light came on.
Mrs Edwards taught us how to make it
For it to work we needed a complete circuit.
We put it together with batteries and wire,
We wrapped it in tinfoil and the temperature got higher.
We had made a mistake but we had spotted it
The tinfoil had made a short circuit

Bryony Cronin, age 8, Sacred Heart School, London

science is just there

science is all around us

we use it every day

we just don't notice it

but it is just there.

opening and closing my desk

is using science again.

Georgina Nicks and Kristieanna Micheala, age 11, Castle Bromwich Junior School, Birmingham

INVENTIONS!

IT IS MY INTENTION TO CREATE A GREAT INVENTION

THE KIND THAT WILL BE COOL JUST LIKE ME AND

EARN ENOUGH MONEY FOR A ROBOTIC BEE OR EVEN A

GARDEN GNOME THAT DID ALL YOUR HOMEWORK BEFORE

YOU GOT HOME

A GNOME THE TEACHERS KNEW YOU NEVER HAD

THEY JUST THOUGHT WOW!

WHAT A CLEVER LAD.

WHAT EVER IT IS, I HOPE IS COOL

SO PEOPLE WILL WRITE BOOKS ABOUT IT

AND READ THEM AT SCHOOL.

Thomas Dodd, age 10, Wilnecote Junior School, Tamworth

My Chocolate Teapot

Have you seen my chocolate teapot?

I left It on the jelly sofa,

Maybe it's playing hide and seek with you and me,

I lost It when I was washing the dishes with petrol,

Where was the strong smell coming from?

When I was standing next to the plastic window,

I was listening to the cotton wool radio.

My dog was eating chunks of iron balls in his waxy candle bowl,

Whilst lapping up caramel syrup.

I was reading my glass cooking book

When my chocolate teapot disappeared!

Shelley Joshi, age 11, Our Lady of Mount Carmel Catholic Primary School, Doncaster

Biotechnology - A cautionary tale about antibiotics

Ever since our evolution, humans have been dying out of the blue
We did not not have any ideas about the causes, until Louis Pasteur gave us a clue
It was about 100 years ago that people started to see why,
Microscopes showed creatures otherwise naked to the human eye.

Human beings began to get cleaner, they scrubbed everything in sight
Fewer people died suddenly, the bugs really got a fright
The population and hospitals were scoured; they built sewers and drains
Everyone was overjoyed, they thought they had such brains.

Then in 1928, Sir Alexander Fleming mad a brilliant mistake
He mixed streptococcus bacteria with mould fungus on a culture plate
The fungus penicillium notatum produced a compound with which the microbes were smothered
Fleming called this compound penicillin and the first antibiotic had been discovered;

After 20 years of extraction and purification, commercial production of antibiotics was pioneered.
New scientific methods to produce desired antibiotics led to organisms that were genetically engineered.
People popped pills and became better, diseases were wiped out,
They did not give a second thought to the germs, they did not have a doubt.

The hospitals are getting dirty once again, as we are all getting lazy,
We should have thought more about the bugs, because they have been very busy
They have survived and grown stronger, as the weaker ones have been killed
The more resistant strains have cross-bred and their little lives have been filled.

Some bacteria pump out antibiotics faster than they can get in,
Others now produce chemicals, which chop-up the deadly poison
Some have developed thicker cell walls, and antibiotics are denied entry
All of the bacteria are fighting back – and they're not very happy.

So the time has now come for everyone to clean up their act
Hospitals need isolation wards and patient screening for resistant
infections, which of late they have lacked
Don 't go dashing to the doctor at the slightest sniffle for a pill
And don't use 'antibacterial' products, good old soap and water
works just as well.

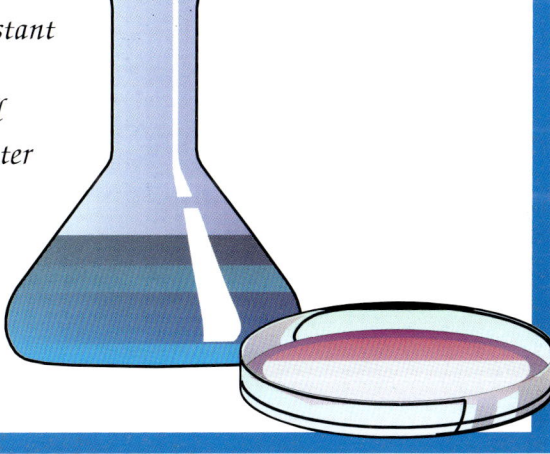

Verity Fryer, age 18, Colyton Grammar School, Devon

The World of Science

Wondering how the flowers grow?
Photosynthesis, you know.

What are genes and what do they do?
They makes the plan that makes you you.

Which is faster sound or light?
Why do opposite magnets fight?

What is a chemical reaction?
Why do prisms cause refraction?

Ovaries can make the seeds,
But earth provides its other needs.

Who'd have thought evaporation,
Was the cause of condensation.

The tilting earth results in seasons,
Day follows night for different reasons.

Want to make sense of the world all around?
Well get into SCIENCE where the answers are found!

Kirsty Dawson, age 11, Stockport Grammar Junior School, Cheshire

The Experiment

The **acid** is on the table,
I have got my **lab coat** on.
I'm ready to start the experiment
I hope nothing will go wrong

for today's research you will need
an **acid** and an **alkali**.
a drop of each **together** will prove,
That **neutralisation** is not a lie.

Suddenly the colour changes,
pH 7 neutral that's green.
and I can now tell all my friends
That a **reaction** is what I've seen.

Olivia Nairn, age 13, James Allen's Girls' School, London

Planet Time!

9 planets rest way up in the sky,
And this is the reason why;
600 million years ago their making begun,
hey were formed from the dust of the sun.

I'm going to take each one,
(Not including the Moon and Sun)
And I hope to teach,
You a little bit about each.

Mercury is quite small,
And is covered in craters which are tall,
Mercury's between Venus and the Sun,
And from Earth it can't be seen by anyone.

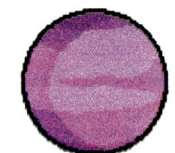

Venus has a dense atmosphere,
So no one on earth could live here,
It takes 243 days on its axis to rotate fully,
It's heavy clouds are very woolly.

Earth has a strong gravitational pull,
And of life forms it is full,
From the sun. the earth reflects light,
And it moves to produce day and night.

Mars is named after the God of War,
Because it wasn't molten for long - it has a small core,
Mars is coloured red and is bold,
But surprisingly it is very cold.

Jupiter is the biggest planet of all,
But has a rocky care which is small,
To rotate on its axis it only takes 10 hours,
Fits fast spin creates winds and giant rain showers.

A day on Saturn would be 10 1/2 hours long,
Its gravitational pull isn't at all very strong,
has such a low density, that on water it could float,
And it can have winds as fast as 1120 mph - I would just like to quote.

Uranus is coloured blue and green,
Through good telescopes, as clouds, it is seen?
It s so cold that you couldn't possibly live there,
And you'd probably get icicles in your hair!

Neptune wasn't discovered until 150 years ago,
The speed of its winds vary from high to low,
Neptune is blue with clouds of white,
And 8 moons it does own at night.

Lastly we have Pluto; Lonely, ice cold and dark,
It's the finest out of the solar system, so the sun looks like a small spark
It's the tiniest planet out of the whole lot,
And from earth it is like a tiny spot.

You to can remember the order of the planets if you say this simple rhyme:

My	Very	Efficient	Memory	Just	Stores	Up	Nine	Planets
E	E	A	A	U	A	R	E	L
R	N	R	R	P	T	A	P	U
C	U	T	S	I	U	N	T	T
U	S	H		T	R	U	U	O
R				E	N	S	N	
Y				R			E	

Lucy Holmes, age 12, Thorpe House School, Norwich

Meteorites are HUGE!

Meteorites are ZOOMING!

Flaming and flaring

Disturbing, destroying

Meteorites are GLOOMING

Meteorites came, dinosaurs GO

Dinosaurs GONE! people GROW!

Joseph Sutherland and friends, age 6 and 7, Stancliffe Hall School, Darley Dale, Derbyshire

SCIENCE

I don't like lessons
And I don't like school
I have to study science
And its Cruel! Cruel! Cruel!

Hydrogen and Oxygen
And water in the air.
Does it really matter
And do I really care?

I know to make the teacher smile
I should sit down and listen
But wait a minute. I'm only ten
And I'd rather be out fishing!

Lewis Tweed, age 10, St John's CE Primary School, Buckhurst Hill, Essex

The Father of Television

John Logie Baird was a young Scotsman
Who had an incredible dream
That one day we would all see pictures
In our own homes, on a screen.
Although a sick man, and also very poor
He worked day in, and day out
On his wash-stand for a workbench
To bring this miracle about.

He used an electric motor from a junk shop
Lenses from cycle lamps, a torch or two
Some parts from a dismantled army radio
Plus string, glue and sealing wax to see him through.
His idea was to send pictures by radio
And for two years he worked at a loss
Of how to complete the transmission
Until he succeeded - with a Maltese Cross.

John Logie Baird then moved to London
And on 30th September 1929 the BBC
Gave its first television broadcast
Using Baird's system, for all to see.
So when you switch on to BBC or ITV
Honour the man to whom we owe a great debt
For with his hard work, and scientific brain
Baird brought to our homes the television set.

Adam Towndrow, age 9, St Anthony's - Leweston Preparatory School, Sherbourne, Dorset

I LOVE SCIENCE

I love Science

It is so cool

I learn about moving objects

When I'm at School

****

How a toy car moves

Going down the slope

With different distances

Not crashing- I hope!

****

I love Science

I love it so

Because with Science

There's lots to know

Tom Simper, age 7, Our Lady Immaculate School, Tolworth, Surrey

THE ECLIPSE

TODAY IS THE DAY
THE WORLD STOOD STILL,
IN THE GARDEN
ON THE STREET
AND ON THE HILL,
EVERYONE'S WATCHING
THE SUN SO BRIGHT,
WAITING FOR THE MOON
TO DIM THE LIGHT,
THE BIRDS STOPPED SINGING
IT'S GONE A LITTLE COLD,
I'M JOINING IN HISTOR Y
A MEMORY TO HOLD,
SILENTLY, SMOOTHLY IT SLIPS
INTO PLACE,
COVERING THE SUNS
BRIGHT ORANGEY FACE,
LOOK ABOVE MY
HEART STARTS TO SING,
I SEE IT
IT'S THERE THE DIAMOND RING!
THE DARKNESS IS LEA VING
THE LIGHTS COMING THROUGH,
MY FIRST TOTAL ECLIPSE

*I SAW ....**IT'S TRUE!***

Jemma Tennant, age 11, East Dene J & I School, Rotherham

The Journey of the Seed

I watch the seed fly silently,
Across the flower scattered meadow,
And as the seed hovers close to me,
I see how it is carefully designed,
And aerodynamic, suited to fly,
It is whisked away by the gentle breeze,
Then other seeds come floating by,
And each have the same qualities,
As the other seed, now far away,
On the soft, rich soil, of the farmer's field.

The soil is full of nutrients,
Which help the plants to grow,
The little seed has caught first glance,
Of its new-found home,
It lands there, in a hole in the ground,
And will lay forgotten, for a long time,
But the plant is busy, under the soil,
Creating a shoot, then a root
And when out of the soft, moist earth,
The plant absorbs the fresh, warm sunlight.

The dandelion's height gradually increased,
And then it shot up like a rocket,
Now the plant had five large, grand leaves,
Each one so green with photosynthesis,
And in June, a huge yellow bud formed,
On the tip of the sturdy, slender stem,
Out opens a magnificent flower,
And the carpel and the stamens are so delicate,
And the petals so frail, yet exquisitely decorated,
To attract insects from near or far.

A swarm of bees come swirling by,
Their hum so sharp and loud,
In a flash, they are gone,
All except one, who settles on the flower,
He hovers, sucking the sweet nectar,
With his long, curly proboscis,
He dives into the flower,
Dusty pollen from his stripy back,
Scrapes onto the sticky stigma,
And the bee glides away.

The pollen is sucked down the style,
And fertilizes eggs to make seeds,
The ovary swells to the size of a pea,
The flower dies, the seeds float away,
On with the journey of a lifetime.

Lizzie Boulden, age 11, Aldington Primary School, Aldington, Kent

Puberty

My chest is getting bigger,
My pubic hair's growing,
My hair is really greasy,
My spots are showing.
'What is happening to me?'
I called to my mum,
She turned and shouted
'Its called puberty, love!'
So that's what it's called,
This thing that's made me like this...
I HATE PUBERTY!

My Sperm is producing,
My Pubic hair's growing,
My voice is getting deeper,
My facial hair's Showing,
'What happening to me?'
I called to my dad,
He turned and shouted,
'Its puberty, lad!'
So that's what it's called,
This thing that makes me like this...
I HATE PUBERTY

Harriet Chatfield, age 12, St Teresa's School, Dorking, Surrey

Life As We Know It or is It Death?

From the sea to the land,
From crawling to running,
    Hanging in trees,
    Typing on PCs,
        Earth versus Office,
        Life against Death,
            Fighting for survival in an urban jungle,
            Where the predators are no longer animals
                But a different sort of animal,
            Muggers and rapists,
                For better or worse,
                Development or freedom?
                  Developing
                  Changing
                      Living
                    Breathing
                        Killing
                        Destroying
                          Greedy
                            Man.

Sarah Taylor, age 15, Thomas Hardye School, Dorchester, Dorset

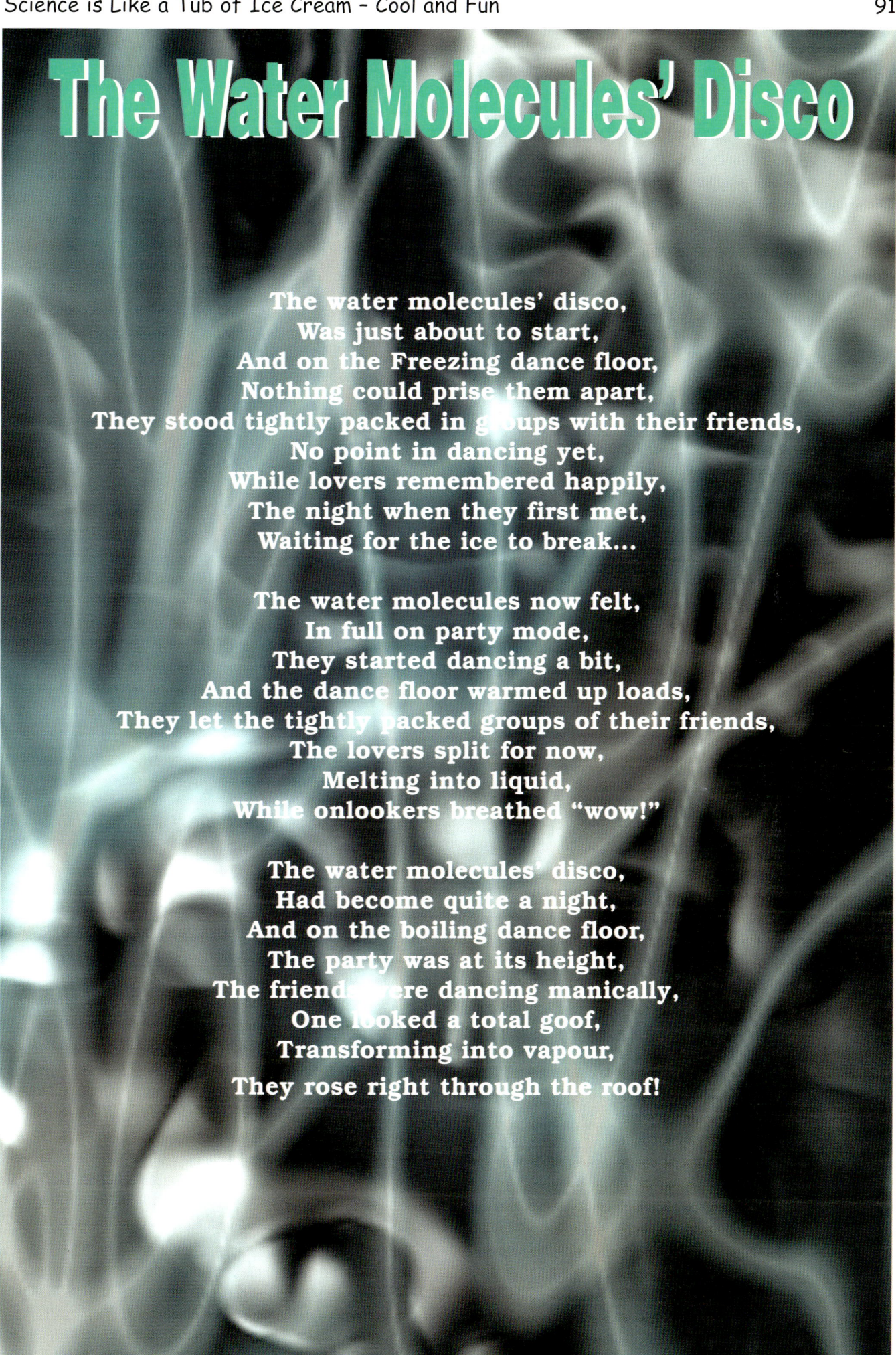

The Water Molecules' Disco

The water molecules' disco,
Was just about to start,
And on the Freezing dance floor,
Nothing could prise them apart,
They stood tightly packed in groups with their friends,
No point in dancing yet,
While lovers remembered happily,
The night when they first met,
Waiting for the ice to break...

The water molecules now felt,
In full on party mode,
They started dancing a bit,
And the dance floor warmed up loads,
They let the tightly packed groups of their friends,
The lovers split for now,
Melting into liquid,
While onlookers breathed "wow!"

The water molecules' disco,
Had become quite a night,
And on the boiling dance floor,
The party was at its height,
The friends were dancing manically,
One looked a total goof,
Transforming into vapour,
They rose right through the roof!

Rachel Evans, age 13, The Earl's High School, Halesowen, West Midlands

THE HUMAN FORMULA

A reaction is a chemical change
Making something new.
A reaction is a human response
Linking and changing people.

Energy cannot be created or destroyed;
Breaking bonds releases energy.
Making bonds requires energy;
Human bonds return energy.

Parallel circuits allow independent components;
Humans work in series, depending on one another
Waves exist as individual frequencies;
Humans work on different wavelengths.

Time is the universal constant,
It imprisons the Universe.
Don't kill time – seize the moment
It will not wait for us.

Light is a transverse wave,
It travels in a straight line,
Distorting our perception –
Reflecting the past.

Pupils from Mrs Turvey's Class, age 15 and 16, Polam Hall School, Darlington, Co. Durham

EVAPORATION POEM

Now the storm is over,
The sky is growing light,
The rain has formed huge puddles,
Sparkling, deep and bright.

The sun begins to shine again,
Warming all the land,
Sucking in the puddles,
Like a straw held in a hand.

Evaporation is the name,
When water in a mass,
Changes its' appearance,
From liquid into gas.

Particles move freely
Vapour is the name,
Floating in the atmosphere,
Up the ladder to fame

Clouds are gathering one more time
Full of liquid rain
Threatening a soaking
The cycle starts again.

Peter Wallace, age 11, Stockport Grammar Junior School, Cheshire

The History of Science

In a far off land that's not yet been explored,
The natives decided, being typically bored,
To teach themselves something, but what was the question,
Not even their god Scie, had the slightest suggestion.
They pondered, they queried, they argued and fought,
But the question remained, Just what should be taught?
Latin? Too complicated. Mathematics? Been done.
Nothing was found that was remotely near fun.
Then up spoke a young lad, Filance was his name,
His idea was outstanding, or so people claim.
Although I'm not sure of the exact words that he spoke,
It was something on the lines of 'This isn't a joke.
If we all work together I'm sure we can find
The solutions to problems of every kind.
There are really no limits, we people aren't fools,
We can work safely if we stick to the rules.'
So from then on the people from that far away land,
Studied devotedly what came to their hand.
From rocks and animals like the mouse and the shrew,
To anatomy, astronomy and wavelengths too.
There was only one problem, What should it be called?
Then Scie, from the heavens, an idea he bawled.
"We'll take 3 letters from Filance," he did yell,
"And all of my name, Now what does that spell?"
After numerous meetings about Filance and Scie,
'Science' was the solution, Lord only knows why!
Many happy years later, resources ran short,
So their options were just about, basically nought.
After leaving their country and waving their last,
Where, of all places, should they chance to sail past.
With shouts of 'oh excellent' and 'look, land ahoy.'
'it's our chance to spread knowledge' 'anchor here' and 'oh boy.'
Some became doctors, some became preachers,
But the majority are now known as our science teachers!

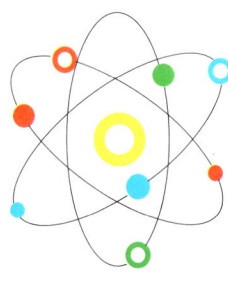

Becky Massen, age 15, Healing Comprehensive School, Grimsby

Last week I was on Snowdon,

High above the ground.

Only steps away from the end.

But now, even more fascinating,

I am being told about the structure,

Of those immense peaks,

How the atoms hold together.

Next time the immensity of it all

Will be much more apparent.

Arran Willis, age 15, The King's School, Ely, Cambridgeshire

Why?

A seagull soars through the air on wings that defy gravity,

It's feathers bristling in the wind from the self-generated current,

It's small beady eyes look upon the great expanse of the sea looking for food,

But not finding any in a now blackened sea.

Another seagull sits on the beach,

Sits among other birds waiting to die,

Their small fragile bodies covered with oil,

Hindering their attempts to fly away from this carnage.

Hours, days, weeks, months past and the damage remains,

Fish killed by the thousands, washed up along the shoreline,

Giving the impression that a delicate experiment between luck and fait was fatally disrupted,

And in all of this, a small simple-minded bird might ask: "why?"

Jason Greer, age 16, Menwith Hill School, Harrogate, North Yorkshire

Food Chain

I sprayed pesticide on my rosebush one day,
To try to clear the greenfly away.
The Ladybird ate them one by one,
Until he had ten greenfly's in his tum.

He then he got eaten by a garden spider,
After getting himself trapped in the web beside her.
She stored the bug in her live food larder,
Which then got fuller and fatter and wider.

But then the spider after eating her meal,
Fell prey herself to a red robin's bill.
The robin sat watching the spider get fat,
But then became dinner to next door's cat.

The cat which had been hiding in a log,
While all the time being watched by a dog.
The dog then chased him long and far
But then the cat was hit by a car.

The cat lay under a bush to die,
And after was visited by a nearby fly,
The fly laid her eggs on the new food supply,
Then happily left her children, bye, bye.

The maggots when hatched ate and munched all day long,
Until came the day all the cat had gone.
Now from their home where their life had started,
They all said goodbye and together they parted.

They crawled into cracks and holes in the ground,
Then changed into fly's that flew all around.
Some flew into houses, in sheds and towers,
Some flew up high and some near flowers.

But all These fly's soon all died,
And all because of the pesticide.
And all the birds that ate them died too,
By pesticide sprayed by me and you.

Ian Clarke, age 12, The Sweyne Park School, Rayleigh, Essex

ELEMENTARY

If a table's periodic then where do you put the chair?
The baffled boffins gathered to debate...
Newton spoke with gravity
As Watt got all steamed up.
Fahrenheit boiled with anger
So Lister washed his hands of it.
"It's all relative," said Einstein calmly,
"Lumiere, try to picture it."
Then Marie Curie saw right through it,
But Boyle put her under pressure,
And Bunsen, typically flamboyant,
Gave Faraday a shock.
"I'm going Ohm," he said,
And slipped away with Freud,
Fleming had the germ of an idea,
Edison shed some light on it,
Marconi broadcast it.
"This is a blast!" declared Von Braun.
Nobel adopted the dynamic approach
While Babbage chipped away at the quest
"That rings a bell," said Alexander G
"A solution is evolving."
"Don't make a monkey of me!" snapped Darwin
So Diesel poured oil on troubled waters.
Logie Baird announced, "It's never black or white-
No more splitting hairs, Mr. Rutherford."
"Eureka!" yelled old Archimedes
"I see it clearly now."
"You're a star," said Galileo.
"Of course!" cried Pascal,
"It's just solids, liquids and gases
So it really does not matter."

Edmond Boullé, age 12, Dulwich College Preparatory School, London

Where do babies come from?

I'm sure when you were very young,
you used to say to dad or mum,
Mummy? Daddy ? Where do babies come from?

Well your mum and dad reply,
And suddenly they go all shy
Well my dear you'll learn some day
how you have turned out this way.

A little creature called a sperm
Which lives inside a man
Will swim towards a tiny egg
As fast as it possibly can.

The egg just waits inside a woman
waiting for a sperm,
it really is quite complicated
there's quite a lot to learn.

The sperm with his little wiggly tail
and its pointy head
finds its way into the egg
while your parents are in bed.

Slowly then the egg splits and grows
as large as it can go,
Then forms into a sort of baby
called an embryo.

The embryo then grows; and grows
and gets all its bits and pieces,
Then it grows a little bit bigger
and this is called a foetus.

In the next nine months your mum gets fat,
starts buying the baby, clothes and hats,
She then goes into hospital
to wait for the baby to be born.

She screams and shouts
While the baby comes out, and daddy holds her hand
Then you give it the name you want
and then you can take it home!

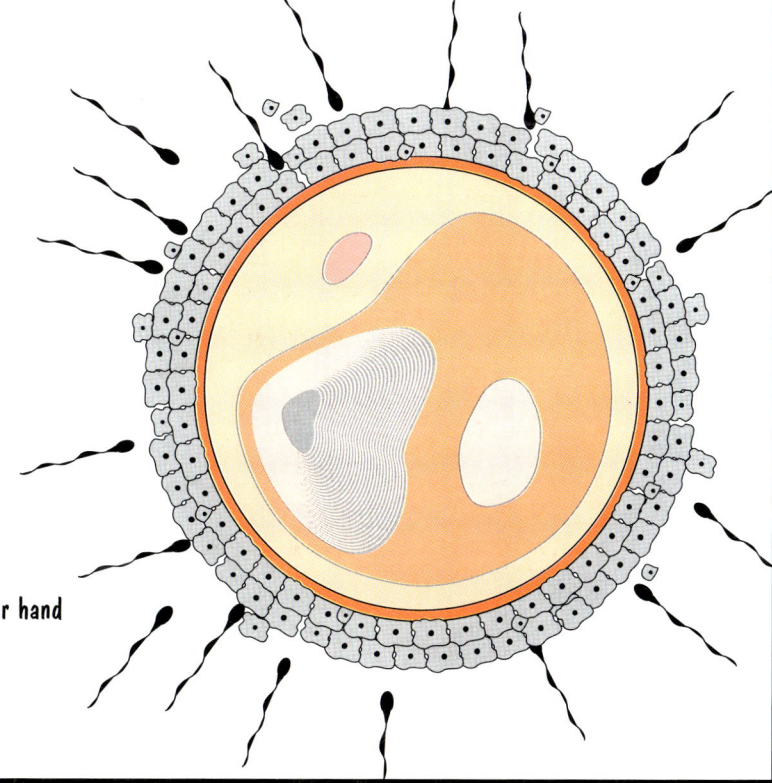

Sarah Flintnam, age 13, Overton Grange School, Sutton, Surrey

SCIENCE!

Science, science, everywhere ,
look at the wall,
look at the chair.

Every day things we see and do
connect to science -
Even me and you.

Difficult science is rockets in space
Easy science is
Wall paper paste.

Science, science everywhere.
This wonderful thing
Is here to share.

Meigan Brown, age 8, Palmers Green High School, London

POLLUTION

Pollution, pollution
Is there a solution?
Our Earth is getting too hot.

Instead of abusing
let's save what we're using
And look after what we have got.

Edward Harker, age 10, St Paul's CE (C) Primary School, Stafford

Equations

No Homework + Science Teacher = TROUBLE
Bomb + Building = RUBBLE

Two Hydrogen + Oxygen = WATER
Mum + Dad = DAUGHTER

Lab + Strong Acid = RUN
Science + Me = FUN

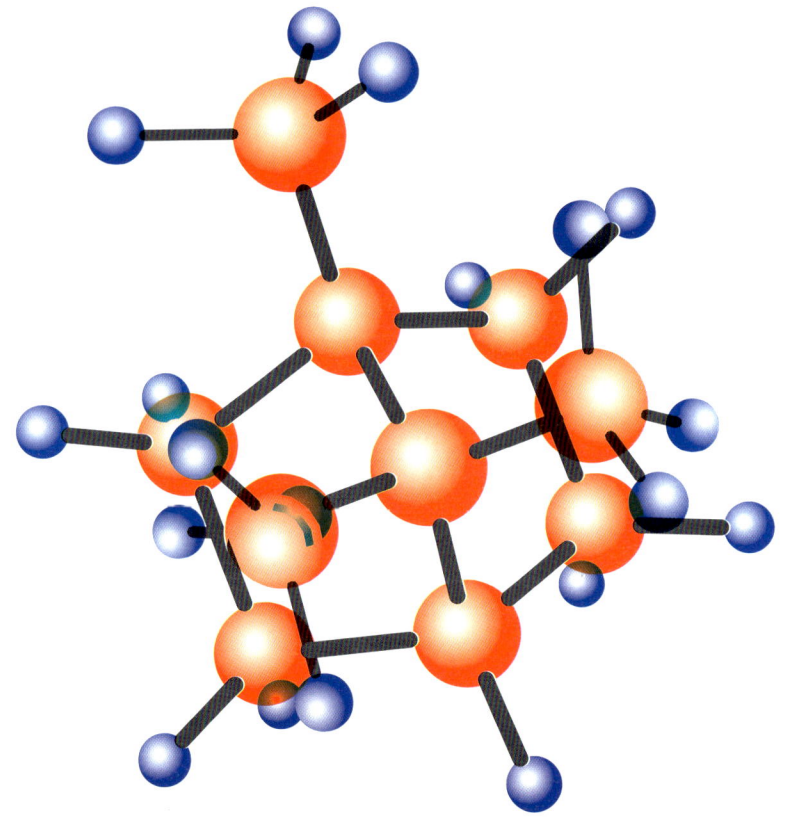

The questions of science

Science,

Now, where shall I begin?

Its all a constant spin,

Helping us to understand,

The secrets of this mysterious land.

All these questions make us dizzy,

The mysteries of science keeps us buzy.

Question after question,

Suggestion after suggestion,

After troubled days and sleepless nights,

Its finally solved, its finally right.

Vicki Blackshaw, age 16, The Kings School, Ely, Cambridgeshire

Science

10   little test tubes sitting in a line,
Gravity made one fall and then there were nine

9   little crystals what is their weight?
One dissolved in water and then there were eight.

8   little batteries wired up to 'Nevin',
He got a shock and then there were seven.

7   little chemicals the children have to mix,
One caused an explosion and then there were six.

6   little plants will they survive?
One didn' t get watered and then there were five.

5   little toy cars pushed towards the door,
Friction did not stop one and then there were four.

4   little flowers pollinated by a bee,
One didn't have a stamen and then there were three.

3   little circuits what do they do?
One didn' t conduct and then there were two.

2   little magnets what can be done?
Repel or attract and then there was one.

One little schoolboy thinks science is so much fun,
He has completed all his experiments and now there are none!

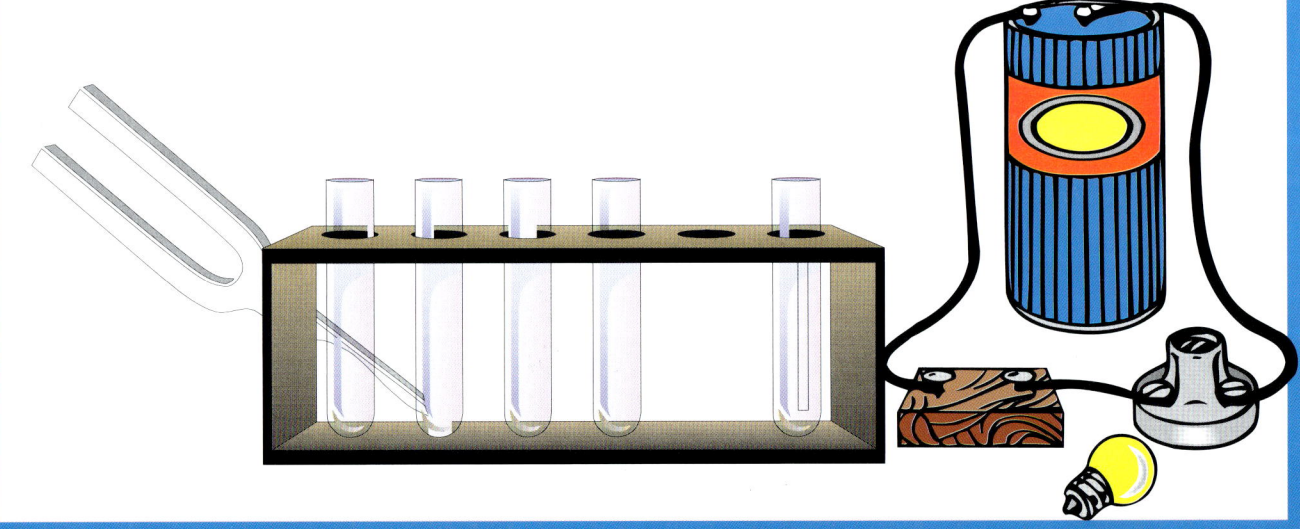

Christopher Walker, age 10, St John's Primary School, Hillsborough, Co. Down, Northern Ireland

The Lab

Pain and terror
disease and torture
the lab
you were born to die
your an experiment
not an animal
no feelings
no love
just an experiment
injections and testing
cages and death
your time has come
they open the door
and reach for you
but you dodge and jump
and your out
you leap through the window
freedom and wildeness
and a gunshot
you feel pain
your legs buckle
and you hit the ground
and your lost
down the dark well of eternity
but at least you died
a free animal

Myra Legg, age 12, The Royal High School, Bath

Space

I am an alien,

and I come from Mars.

Its really quite boring

Without any cars.

Instead it has craters,

Which are big funny holes.

You won't find them normal,

and their aren't any moles.

There's lots of sand

and red rock too,

It's really quite lovely,

especially the view.

I can see the other planets,

orbiting the sun.

Seems like a race,

and having fun.

Yvanna Kurlak, age 9, St Teresa's RC Primary School, Aspley, Nottingham

Genetic Engineering - a cautionary tale
(read in Roald Dahl, Oompa-Loompa style)

My old friend, Miss Mary Greering,
Thought she'd be clever and try genetic engineering.
So she searched the world, heaven and hell,
To find a rare, elusive cell.
When she finally found it on a far off shore
It would she thought, open the door
To fame and fortune, money and wealth,
She never thought it would end her health.
First she removed the cell and with ultrasound,
Jiggled the insides all around.
With mRNA and reverse transcriptase,
She suddenly found she had it all backways.
DNA polymerase chain reaction,
Now she was really seeing some action.
After mixing, annealing and ligase enzyme,
She sat down to wait for a very long time.
There were gurglings and gruntings inside the tube
And suddenly out jumped a Giant Grube.
Its teeth were purple in its ferocious smile,
Ant it's breath smelt ab-so-lutely vile.
How could such a horrid creature,
That wouldn't even be allowed to feature
On Jerry Springer, have come
From that small cell on Mary's bum,
(which is where she eventually found it,
although the authorities wouldn't allow it.)
What Mary didn't know,
That bum DNA when allowed to grow,
In a jiggled up, unnatural state,
Actually flung right wide the gate,
That let out creatures foul and wide,
That made poor Mary want to hide.
This Giant Grube, this horrid beast,
Decided to make its first feast,
Its loyal creator, Frankenstein style,
Though Mary had meant well all the while.
Dear friends, now the beast is free and loose,
Blame old Mary, the silly goose,
And notice with more than a passing nod
That its terribly foolish to try and play God.

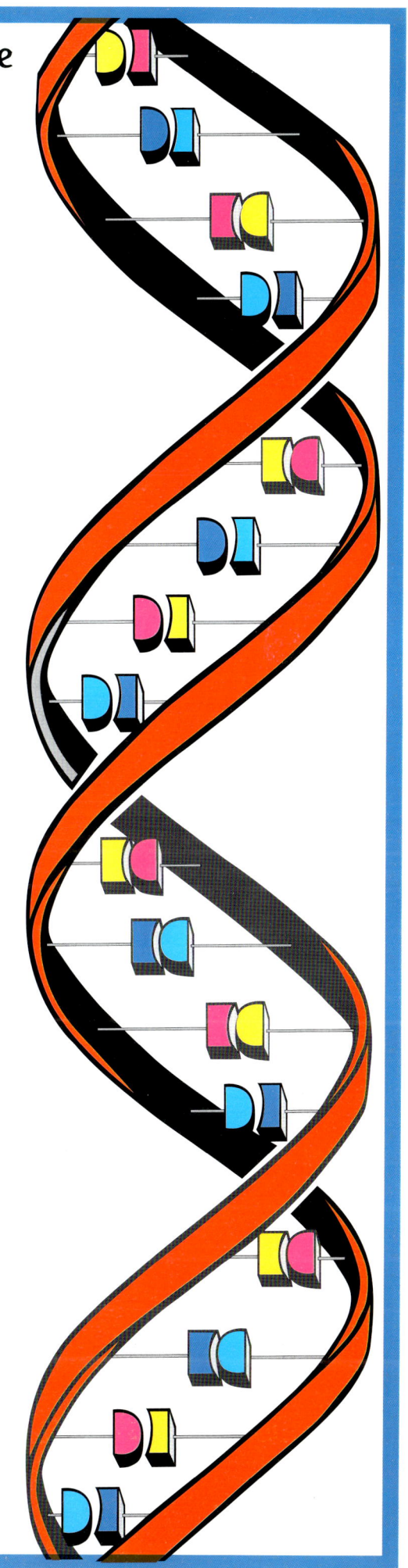

Kate Harris, age 17, Colyton Grammar School, Colyton, Devon

INDEX

INDEX